FAMOUS LIVES

The Story of
BABE RUTH
Baseball's Greatest Legend

FAMOUS LIVES
titles in Large-Print Editions:

FAMOUS LIVES

The Story of
BABE RUTH
Baseball's Greatest Legend

By Lisa Eisenberg

Gareth Stevens Publishing
MILWAUKEE

The author wishes to thank Robert W. Creamer,
author of Babe, *the definitive biography of Babe Ruth,*
for his editorial assistance and advice.

For a free color catalog describing Gareth Stevens Publishing's list of high-quality books and multimedia programs, call 1-800-542-2595 (USA) or 1-800-461-9120 (Canada). Gareth Stevens Publishing's Fax: (414) 225-0377. See our catalog, too, on the World Wide Web: http://gsinc.com

Library of Congress Cataloging-in-Publication Data

Eisenberg, Lisa.
    The story of Babe Ruth: baseball's greatest legend / by Lisa Eisenberg.
       p. cm. — (Famous lives)
    Includes index.
    Summary: Examines the life, career, and personality of the famous baseball player.
    ISBN 0-8368-1486-X (lib. bdg.)
    1. Ruth, Babe, 1895-1948—Juvenile literature. 2. Baseball players—United States—Biography—Juvenile literature. [1. Ruth, Babe, 1895-1948. 2. Baseball players.] I. Title. II. Series: Famous lives (Milwaukee, Wis.)
GV865.R8E57   1997
796.357'092—dc21
   [B]   97-689

The events described in this book are true. They have been carefully researched and excerpted from authentic biographies, writings, and commentaries. No part of this biography has been fictionalized. To learn more about Babe Ruth, refer to the list of books and videos at the back of this book, or ask your librarian to recommend other fine books and videos.

First published in this edition in North America in 1997 by
Gareth Stevens Publishing
1555 North RiverCenter Drive, Suite 201
Milwaukee, Wisconsin 53212 USA

Original © 1990 by Parachute Press, Inc., as a Yearling Biography. Published by arrangement with Bantam Doubleday Dell Books for Young Readers, a division of Bantam Doubleday Dell Publishing Group, Inc. Additional end matter © 1997 by Gareth Stevens, Inc.

Cover illustrated by Chet Jezierski

The trademark Yearling® is registered in the U.S. Patent and Trademark Office.
The trademark Dell® is registered in the U.S. Patent and Trademark Office.

Printed in the United States of America

1 2 3 4 5 6 7 8 9 01 00 99 98 97

Contents

"I Was a Bad Kid"

The Sultan of Swat. The Home Run King. The Bambino. The Babe. These are just *some* of the nicknames given to the great Babe Ruth. In the world of baseball, many legends come and go. But the legend of the great Babe Ruth is here to stay. Today, more than fifty years after he retired from baseball and more than forty years after his death, almost *everybody* knows who he was. Baseball lovers everywhere still tell and retell famous stories about the incredible Babe Ruth. In the hearts of his fans, the Babe's legend lives on—and continues to grow.

What is it that makes the Babe Ruth story so different from any other baseball story? Anyone who knew the Babe as a young boy would never have guessed that he would grow up to be one of the best players who ever lived. In fact, most people who knew him probably would have predicted a future of anything *but* fame and fortune.

George Herman Ruth, Jr.—later known as Babe—was born in a poor, run-down section of Baltimore. For most of his life, Babe Ruth believed he had been born on February 7, 1894. But when he was a grown man he received some legal papers that said he had been born on February 6, 1895. No one knew for sure which was his real birth date, so Babe Ruth continued to celebrate the February 7 date since that was when he'd always celebrated.

"Little George's" father, "Big George," had many different jobs during his life. At the time Babe was born, Big George was working at the Ruth family's grocery store and saloon on Frederick Avenue, near the waterfront. It was in this store and bar that Little George first played and started to walk.

The first few years of Little George's life were fairly happy and comfortable. His parents and his grandparents helped take care of him, and the family business provided enough money for the things they needed.

But when George was five, his father moved the family a few blocks away and started another business, selling lightning rods. When that failed, the Ruths moved again, and Big George opened up his own bar. Little George lived with his mother and father in an apartment upstairs over the saloon. It was then that Little George's life began to change.

"I was a bad kid," Babe Ruth wrote many years later. He said that when he looked back on his childhood, he couldn't really remember whether he knew the difference between right and wrong. Given the kind of place where the Ruths were living, this wasn't very surprising.

The new saloon was in a very rough neighborhood, and there was no one around to keep an eye on George. George's parents weren't able to pay very much attention to him because they were busy trying to run the new business. Before long, Little George was spending most of his time running through alleys, skipping school, and throwing rotten eggs at truckdrivers.

To make matters worse, George's mother, Kate Schamberger Ruth, was sick, tired and unhappy almost all the time. She had eight children, but only George and his little sister, Mary Margaret, called Mamie, survived. When George grew up, he realized that he'd hardly even known his own parents. He felt that this had given him a tough beginning in life.

Although Little George didn't see much of his own parents, he visited his mother's parents from time to time. George thought of his visits with Grandpa and Grandma Schamberger as some of the happiest times of his childhood. Because both the Schambergers and the Ruths spoke German in their homes, George learned that language when he was a young boy. The English he knew he picked up from the tough kids in the street as they stole apples, ran away from the "coppers," and experimented with chewing tobacco and even drinking whiskey together.

Babe Ruth later claimed that he had been a bum when he was a kid. But his sister Mamie didn't agree with him. She claimed that George wasn't really bad—just full of mischief. He was hard to control and he couldn't resist a dare. If you dared him to do something, you could consider it done.

Though many adults might not have approved of the way Little George was brought up, George himself enjoyed his rough life near the waterfront. Running free in the streets was exciting. There was almost always something to do. In fact, it was in the back alleys of the waterfront neighborhood that George played his first pickup games of baseball. They were informal games played with whatever neighborhood children happened to be around. Baseball was a very popular game in many city neighborhoods at that time. Whenever someone in George's family wanted to find him, all they had to do was look for the nearest baseball game.

Little George's biggest problem growing up was that he hated going to school. Busy and tired as they were, his parents did try to make him go. But George simply refused and often played hooky.

George's unsupervised life went on in this way until he was about eight years old. No one knows what might have become of him if he had been allowed to run wild forever. And no one is quite sure what finally happened to bring about the change. One story says there was a gunfight in Big George's saloon one day, and someone called the police. When the police came to the bar, they learned that a young boy was living there. To make matters worse, they heard that the boy constantly got into trouble, almost never went to school, and didn't have the slightest idea how to read or write.

There are different stories about what happened next. According to one, the police called in the city authorities and asked them to find a better place for George to live. But another story says that George's parents finally recognized that they really couldn't take care of their son on their own. Whatever the cause, it was the beginning of a big change for George Herman Ruth.

In 1902, George was sent to live at St. Mary's Industrial School, which was a school for boys who, for different reasons, had problems living at home. When he was gone, his mother missed him and wanted him home again. So his first stay at St. Mary's lasted only one month. But when he returned home, there were problems again and later that year, his father sent him back to St. Mary's for another month. After that, George's family tried to have him live with them at home once more. He lived with his parents for the next two years, but in the end, it didn't work out. George was too wild and too unruly for his parents to handle, especially since Mrs. Ruth was ill so much of the time. In addition to stealing and playing hooky, some stories say that George was already drinking alcohol at the age of nine or ten!

At last, in 1904 when George was ten, he was sent to St. Mary's school for good. Sending their son away wasn't an easy decision for George's parents to make. George's mother cried and changed her

16

mind time and again, knowing how much she would miss her son. But in spite of his parents' doubts, George was finally put on the trolley for the ride to St. Mary's. He stayed at the school, off and on, until he was almost twenty years old.

St. Mary's School

St. Mary's Industrial School for Boys was just outside the city of Baltimore. It stood on a small hill that looked much greener and more country-like than anything Little George had ever seen. When George came to the school to live there permanently, he felt lonely and homesick. Although the surroundings were pleasant, the six three-story gray buildings that made up the school looked big and unfriendly. George missed his family and the life he knew back in the city.

It took George a while to get used to being away from home. At first, he didn't fit in at all. There were eight hundred boys at St. Mary's, and he was one of the youngest. Because he had skipped school so often, he couldn't read or write some of the easiest letters or numbers. He had to go to classes with the youngest boys to catch up, and this made him feel awkward and embarrassed.

St. Mary's was run by the Xaverian Brothers. "Brothers" were men who had taken a vow to lead a religious life. Their lives were similar to those of Catholic priests and nuns. St. Mary's was a Catholic school, but it took in boys of all religions from many different backgrounds. Some of the boys were orphans, others had been in trouble with the police, and others, like George, came from families that just couldn't cope with them.

Life at St. Mary's wasn't easy. The boys had to go to bed at eight o'clock each night and get up by six the next morning. By seven-thirty, they had already gotten washed and dressed, gone to mass, eaten breakfast, and started their classes. There were only about thirty brothers to watch over eight hundred boys. The brothers were kind, but they were strict, too.

One of the brothers George admired the most was Brother Matthias. He was a tall, strong man who, like the other brothers, wore a long, flowing black robe with a sash around the middle. All of the boys were in awe of Brother Matthias's size and strength. They nicknamed him the "Boss." One of George's classmates at St. Mary's said that Brother Matthias, "gave everyone a fair break but, brother, if you ever crossed him you sure were in trouble."

One story about George's years at St. Mary's tells about a fight he had with a new boy at the school. Apparently, George asked the boy to play ball, and the boy started a fist fight. Some other boys joined in, but as soon as they saw Brother Matthias, the fighting stopped at once. Brother Matthias actually picked up the new boy and carried him away! The next day, when the boy came outside, he and George *did* play a game of catch. Somehow, Brother Matthias had convinced the boy to try to get along with everyone. And George was usually willing to forgive and forget.

In addition to classwork, the brothers devoted many hours to teaching the boys values, such as honesty and caring for other people. As he grew up at St. Mary's, Babe developed strong feelings of sympathy and affection for younger, weaker boys. He would hold on to these feelings after he left the school and spend much of his adult life visiting orphanages.

The brothers at St. Mary's worked hard to teach the boys a useful trade so that they would be able to find jobs when they grew up and left school. George learned carpentry, but spent most of his time working in the tailor shop, where he learned to put collars on shirts. After working hard all day, he bought bags of treats from the candy shop that opened in the outside yard each evening after supper.

George loved stuffing himself with sweet snacks. But he was also generous with his candy, freely giving it away to the younger boys who couldn't buy any of their own. Loving sweets and rich food and being generous to other people were characteristics for which the great Babe Ruth would one day be famous.

In addition to the candy hour, the afternoon and Sunday also became special to George. That is when the boys played sports. St. Mary's students played almost every kind of game, including volleyball, basketball, and ice skating. But the most important one was baseball.

George hadn't been at St. Mary's very long before Brother Matthias noticed how well he could play baseball. When Babe Ruth grew up, he recalled how Brother Matthias had noticed his unusual ability for catching and throwing a baseball. He used to take George to one side of the yard at

St. Mary's to practice. There he helped George correct his mistakes with his stance or with how he was holding the bat.

George learned a lot about hitting a baseball from Brother Matthias. While George watched, Brother Matthias would toss up a baseball with one hand and swing the bat with the other. He hit the longest fly balls George had ever seen. Years later, the Babe said he was destined to be a hitter the day he first saw Brother Matthias hit.

Before long, George and the other boys were playing ball almost every chance they got. George developed into such a good baseball player so quickly that almost from the beginning of his stay at the school, he was playing with boys who were several years older than he was. When he was eight or nine, he was already playing with the children who were twelve. By the time he was twelve, he was playing with the sixteen-year-olds. When he'd reached the age of sixteen, he was playing on the best teams the school had to offer.

The eight hundred boys at St. Mary's were organized into about forty different baseball teams. When Babe was about sixteen, he played with a team called the Red Sox. Though he could play many different positions, he was usually catcher.

But then, during a game between the Red Sox and another team, Brother Matthias decided to try an experiment.

George's team was losing, and after a while, George started laughing and poking fun at his own team's pitcher. "All right, George," Brother Matthias said suddenly. "*You* pitch!"

George was astounded. "I don't know how to pitch!" he protested.

But Brother Matthias insisted that if George knew enough to make fun of another pitcher, he knew enough to pitch for himself. The brother was planning to teach smart-aleck George a lesson in humility, but unfortunately, the lesson backfired. "I don't really know how to do this," George said to himself as he hurled his first strike. "But it feels natural."

During his last two years at St. Mary's, George switched from catching to pitching. He got better at pitching—and at hitting, too. During his final season at the school, he was hitting a home run in practically every single game. In one season with the St. Mary's Red Sox, he hit an incredible sixty home runs!

Soon George was playing so well, he was being written up in the local newspapers. St. Mary's gave him permission to leave the school on weekends to play with other teams. Before long, Jack Dunn, the owner and manager of a minor league team called the Baltimore Orioles, started hearing rumors about the new young star at St. Mary's School. In 1913, Dunn came to St. Mary's to watch George pitch in a game against Mount St. Joseph's College.

St. Joseph's was one of St. Mary's biggest rivals, and they had a good team. Their pitcher, Morrisette, was so good that he was being considered for a position in professional baseball.

To get ready for the game, the entire school was cleaned and swept. Flags were put up all over the grounds. When the big day finally came, a noisy crowd showed up to watch.

Another boy might have felt the pressure of the crowd and become nervous, but not George Ruth. He went to the mound and struck out twenty-two St. Joseph batters! The final score of the game was St. Mary's 6, St. Joseph's 0. The St. Mary's boys were wild with joy, and so was George.

Immediately after the game, George, Jack Dunn, Brother Matthias, and two other brothers from St. Mary's all went into the school office for a conference. Jack Dunn thought George was so good that he offered him a position as a pitcher for the Orioles! But there was one big problem: George was under twenty-one—too young to sign a contract. At first, there seemed no way out of the situation, but then one of the brothers came up with a solution.

When Babe was thirteen, his mother had died of tuberculosis. Even though George's father was still alive, he was no longer responsible for his son. When George entered St. Mary's permanently, one of the brothers, Brother Paul, was made George's legal guardian. That meant he had the authority to give Jack Dunn official permission to be in charge of George until the boy was twenty-one years old. Everyone agreed that this was the best way to work out the problem.

George couldn't believe his good luck. Mr. Dunn was going to pay him six hundred dollars to play with his team! To George that seemed like all the money in the world. As he picked up the pen to sign the contract, he smiled from ear to ear.

On a cold winter day in 1914, nineteen-year-old George packed up his things and got ready to leave St. Mary's. The day wasn't an easy one for him. Although he was excited about playing with the Orioles, St. Mary's was the only real home he'd ever had. He had many friends there, and he regarded some of the brothers as his family. He felt especially sorry about saying good-bye to Brother Matthias, whom he would later describe as the greatest man he had ever known.

St. Mary's had tremendously affected George's life. During his years there, he'd grown from a lonely little boy to a powerful, muscular young man. He still had the same loud, brash, reckless personality he'd had all his life. But now he also had an enormous grin and an easygoing charm. He had developed warm feelings for other people, particularly younger children who were less fortunate than he was, like the boys he shared his candy with in the schoolyard.

On February 27, George said his last good-bye and walked out the front gates of the school. Although he'd never come back as a student at St. Mary's, he would come back as a visitor many times for the rest of his life. He would never forget the school or what it had done for him. "I'm proud of St. Mary's," he said when he grew up. "I will be happy to bop anybody on the beezer who speaks ill of it."

Pro Ball

After he left St. Mary's, George went home to spend a weekend with his father back at the saloon in Baltimore. That weekend, a terrible snow storm struck. High winds blew, and a foot of snow fell. By Monday morning, the city streets were filled with snow, tree branches, and broken glass. Most people stayed in their homes, looking out the window at the storm's damage.

George was different. Nothing was going to stop him from getting to the hotel where he was supposed to meet the rest of the Orioles' team. Some of the players were stranded and didn't make it to the hotel, but George was right on time. He and the other team members who had managed to get through the snow went to Union Station and climbed onto the train bound for Fayetteville, North Carolina, and spring training.

George was thrilled to be taking his first train ride. When some of the older players saw how excited he was, they decided to have a little fun with him. They showed him the upper berth, or bunk, where he would sleep that night. Then they pointed out a small cloth sling hanging on the wall above the berth. "It's to put your pitching arm in while you sleep, George," they said, hiding their smiles behind their hands. The sling was actually designed as a resting place for a passenger's clothes. But no one let George in on the joke for the rest of the ride. He spent a long, uncomfortable night on the train trying to sleep with his arm hanging up over his head!

It was in Fayetteville, at spring training, that people first started calling George Ruth "Babe." There are several stories about where the nickname came from. One says that George had so much fun riding up and down on the hotel elevator in Fayetteville that someone called him a "babe in the woods," meaning that he was acting like a young, inexperienced child. Another story says that a player spotted George with Jack Dunn and called out, "Look at Dunnie and his new babe!"

Babe himself said the name might have had its origins in the Fayetteville hotel dining room. When George sat down to breakfast the first morning, another player told him he could order whatever he wanted to eat—and the baseball club would pay for all of it. George was overjoyed! Years later, he wrote about how he'd been busily eating three stacks of wheatcakes and three stacks of ham when he suddenly realized that some of the other players were staring at him. Then one of the players laughed and said George was just like a big baby or a babe. And from that moment on, George Ruth was known as the Babe.

People still talk about Babe Ruth's first day as a pro, or professional, ball player in Fayetteville. In his first time up at bat, Babe didn't do anything special. But when he came up for a second chance, Babe hit an amazing home run. The ball flew farther than anyone in town had ever seen a ball go. Babe made it all the way to home plate before the fielder even *found* the ball in the cornfield!

Babe got a chance to pitch the last two innings of that game, and his team won, 15–9. Jack Dunn broke into a grin. He had been right about the young boy from St. Mary's!

After that, on most days, Dunn praised Babe to

anyone who would listen. There was one time, however, when he lost his temper with his new player. Although Babe was already acting like an experienced player on the baseball field, off the field, he acted like the great big kid he still was. He was still thrilled about how much he could eat at the ballclub's expense, and soon the other players were all making jokes about how much Babe could eat.

One day, Babe was out on a bicycle ride. As he sped in and out through the streets near the ballpark, he almost crashed right into Dunn himself! After a dramatic fall, Babe sat on the ground and grinned up at his manager. Dunn shook his head and rolled his eyes toward the sky. He couldn't help wondering if Babe would *ever* grow up!

But despite Babe's behavior off the baseball field, he played well in spring training. By the time training was over and the team returned to Baltimore, the fans had already begun to talk about him. Unfortunately, Babe had a few disappointments in Baltimore. The fans weren't coming to see the games. Instead, they were going across the street to watch the Terrapins, a team that was part of a different league.

Jack Dunn was hoping that people might hear about how good Babe was and come to see him play, but the fans just didn't respond. In April, when Babe pitched an exciting six-hitter against the Buffalo Bisons, most of the stands were empty.

In spite of the low fan turnout, Babe began pitching better and better. He was important to the team, and he knew it. This made him feel good. He enjoyed traveling with the Orioles on away games and seeing the country. But, while his pitching continued to improve, his hitting was often poor. This is probably because, at the time, Babe was just beginning to develop his powerful style of batting. This "big swing" of Babe's would one day become famous, but for now, it often made him strike out at the plate.

Nonetheless, Babe's pitching was brilliant. But this wasn't enough to save the Orioles. Jack Dunn had been having problems all season because the fans were just not coming to watch the Orioles play. Dunn was losing money on the team. Finally, he had to face the truth. He would have to sell his best players to major league teams in order to make some money to keep his team going.

In the middle of the 1914 season, the Orioles' manager sold some players to the New York Yankees and the Cincinnati Reds. Finally, on July 10, he sold three more players to the Boston Red Sox. Babe Ruth was one of them.

Babe felt sad about leaving Baltimore, since it was the only place he'd ever lived. But he felt excited, too. He had played for the Orioles for only five months. Now he was going to play for the Red Sox and be in the major leagues!

Welcome to Boston

When Babe got to Boston, he was six feet two inches tall and weighed 190 pounds. He was much larger than the average ballplayer of that time. Babe liked Boston. Almost as soon as he arrived in town, he fell in love with a pretty young waitress named Helen Woodford. She worked in Lander's Coffee Shop. Soon he was spending a lot of his time—and a lot of his newly earned money—going out with Helen and enjoying his new life in the major leagues.

But the 1914 season wasn't an especially happy one for Babe, mostly because he didn't get to play a lot of baseball. The Red Sox manager, Bill Carrigan, let Babe pitch in a few games, but he didn't seem to be impressed with Babe's pitching or his hitting. One story says that's because Babe developed a bad habit at this time. Whenever he threw a curveball, he would curl his tongue into the corner of his mouth. Batters for the opposing teams soon noticed this habit. And whenever they saw Babe's tongue curl, they got set to smack a curveball. Carrigan, who was sometimes called "Rough" for the way he'd played baseball, ordered Babe to get over this habit—or ruin his career as a pitcher.

Carrigan had used Babe as a pitcher almost as soon as he came to Boston. Then, for almost a month, Carrigan didn't let Babe pitch or play in a game at all.

No one is sure why Babe wasn't given more of a chance to play during his first season. One reason may have been the curling tongue, but another possibility was Babe's personality. He often joked around and showed off on the field, but his Red Sox teammates didn't always think he was funny. He could be loud, obnoxious, and abrasive, and some of the other players couldn't get used to his behavior.

Whatever the reason, in August of that year, Carrigan made a decision Babe didn't like at all. He sent Babe to play for the Grays, the Red Sox's minor league team in Providence, Rhode Island, for the rest of the season. This decision was a great disappointment to Babe. He had just gotten started in the major leagues. Why was Carrigan shipping him back to the minors?

Babe's feelings were hurt, but he played hard and pitched nine winning games. With Babe's help, the Grays won their league's pennant. His batting average with the Grays was .300. It wasn't the major leagues, but it was certainly an impressive start for a rookie.

At the end of that season, Babe decided to go back to Baltimore for a while. But there was one thing he had to do first. He went back to Lander's Coffee Shop in Boston to see the waitress, Helen Woodford. "Hon, how about you and me getting married?" he asked her.

Helen stared at the Babe in surprise. She hadn't known him very long, and she was still very young. But, without waiting too long, she smiled at him and said, "Yes!" Babe and Helen were married in Baltimore in October of 1914. The Ruth family gave them a party at the saloon afterwards, and Babe and Helen stayed in Baltimore for the rest of the winter.

*   *   *

The spring of 1915 found Babe back on the Red Sox team again. Even though he was now twenty years old, he was still a brash, innocent kid. He loved practical jokes and kidding around, and he didn't like following rules.

Babe had a lot to learn about getting along with other people. He was so difficult, Carrigan had trouble finding anyone on the team who was willing to be Babe's roommate! Later in his life, Babe recalled a story about his first roommate, Ernie Shore. Ernie had been Babe's teammate when they played for the Orioles. But after just a few weeks of rooming with Babe, Ernie went to Carrigan to complain. Ernie told the manager he would leave the club unless he could have a different roommate! One of the main reasons Ernie wanted the change was that Babe was using his toothbrush. But when Ernie complained to Babe about it, Babe said, "That's all right, Ernie. I'm not particular!" Years later, Babe admitted that he had helped to put a few gray hairs on Carrigan's head that season!

At the beginning of the 1915 season, Babe still wasn't Carrigan's first choice as a pitcher. The manager had started Babe in one game but he didn't look good at all. Babe found himself back in his old familiar place—on the bench. But later on in the season, when another pitcher got hurt, Carrigan *had* to use Babe.

By mid-summer Babe's pitching improved dramatically. The team's playing improved, too, and by July, they were in a race for the pennant with Chicago and Detroit.

At about this time, people were also beginning to notice how well Babe could hit the ball. Some sportswriters suggested that Carrigan should give Babe more opportunity to hit. But Babe continued to concentrate on his pitching that year.

The 1915 season was an exciting one for Babe. It was a time he would remember for his entire life. For one thing, it was his first real season with the Red Sox, and he was thrilled just to be a part of a major league team again. For another, he was now earning more money than he'd ever dreamed of, and it gave the poor boy from the streets of Baltimore a great feeling. But the best reason was that the pennant race was getting more interesting. By August, the Detroit Tigers and the Red Sox were in a neck-and-neck race to see who would win. It was just the kind of hard-fighting, competitive situation Babe Ruth thrived on.

At the end of the season, after a long battle, the Red Sox won the pennant and moved on to the World Series. Babe was proud of the eighteen winning games he had pitched during the season. When the Red Sox met the Philadelphia Phillies in the World Series, Babe couldn't wait to get on the mound and pitch some more winners. But he didn't get the chance.

"I ate my heart out on the bench in that Series," Babe wrote in his autobiography. "I was the American League's won-and-lost leader, and I naturally expected to pitch."

Babe grabbed Carrigan before each game of the Series and asked when he would be pitching. But instead of using Babe, the Red Sox manager decided to rely on some of his other brilliant pitchers, like Ernie Shore. In the first game, Carrigan sent Babe in to pinch-hit for Ernie, but unfortunately, Babe was thrown out at first base. When he got back to the dugout, he shook his head and said he wished he'd been able to hit that one. Shore, who ended up being the losing pitcher in the game, shook his head, and said he wished the very same thing!

Fortunately for the team, however, that was the only game in the Series the Red Sox lost. They won the next four games and became the World Champions! Babe forgot his disappointment at not playing and joined in the celebrations with the other players. It felt wonderful just to be a member of a team that had played so well.

A Big Season for the Babe

In spite of their great success in 1915, Babe Ruth and the Red Sox got off to a slow start in the first few months of the 1916 season. Their loyal fans groaned, but they encouraged their team to get out there and start playing some real baseball! Before long, both Babe's pitching and hitting began to pick up. And by June, things were turning around for the Red Sox.

Though he had yet to become an outstanding hitter, Babe did hit three home runs in the 1916 season. And by August, his pitching was really outstanding. By the end of the season, he'd won twenty-three games, including nine shutouts.

The World Series that year was between the Red

Sox and the Brooklyn Dodgers. Babe didn't get to pitch in the first game in Boston. The great Ernie Shore pitched and won. But for the second game of the Series, Manager Carrigan chose Babe to pitch. No one knew then that this game would go down in baseball history. In fact, at the start of the game, many people wondered if it might not be called off because of rain.

When Babe began pitching, his hopes were high. He gave up a run in the first inning and batted in a run in the third to tie the score, 1–1.

Six long innings later, in the bottom of the ninth, the score was still tied 1–1! Both teams had missed several chances to score more runs, and the players had gotten into a few arguments. The fans were wild with excitement.

When both teams failed to score in the ninth, the game went into extra innings. After such a long, hard game, the Dodger pitcher started to look tired—but not Babe. He felt better and stronger with each pitch.

The game went on, and still no one scored. It went into the tenth inning, then the eleventh, twelfth, and thirteenth. By the fourteenth inning, it was almost too dark to see. Then, finally, in the bottom of the fourteenth, though they could barely see the ball, a Red Sox player smacked a hit into left field and drove in a run. The Red Sox had finally won! It was a great win for the team. But for Babe Ruth, it was a great personal victory as well. Fourteen innings was the longest World Series game in history. And Babe had pitched the entire game and won it!

Babe was so excited, he jumped and shouted and ran around the clubhouse. "I told you I could do it!" he yelled at Manager Bill Carrigan. "I told you I could beat those bums!"

Carrigan grinned and agreed with him. He was as happy as the Babe about winning the game, but he was also a little sad. A few months earlier, Carrigan had told the Red Sox he would be retiring as their manager at the end of the 1916 season. Only days later, when the Red Sox clinched the Series four games to one, he went out onto the field and waved a last good-bye to the Boston fans. Even though their relationship hadn't always been a smooth one, for the rest of Babe Ruth's life he would refer to Bill Carrigan as the greatest manager he'd ever known.

After the end of the World Series, Babe went off on a vacation in New Hampshire with Helen and some of their friends. For the first time in his life,

Babe Ruth goes to bat for Easter Seals, with children from the Florida Association for Crippled Children and Adults.

Babe Ruth; his first wife, Helen Woodford; and their child, Dorothy.

Babe Ruth and a young friend demonstrate the winning stance.

Babe Ruth and members of the famous 1927 Yankees.
From left to right: Waite Hoyt, Babe Ruth, Miller Huggins,
Bob Meusel, and Bob Shawkey.

Babe Ruth takes time out to autograph a baseball during the 1924 season.

Babe Ruth is greeted at home plate by Lou Gehrig after hitting his historic 60th home run.

Babe Ruth scores during the first game of the doubleheader between the New York Yankees and the Detroit Tigers at Yankee Stadium, August 14, 1934.

Babe Ruth and his second wife, Claire Merritt Hodgson, on vacation in Palm Beach.

Before teeing off, Babe and his friends discuss the fine points of Babe's second favorite game.

Babe Ruth celebrates his 39th birthday with a special cake sent by one of his fans.

Babe Ruth leans on a bat during his farewell ceremony, June 1948.

The New York Yankees and thousands of fans observe a moment of silence after hearing of Babe Ruth's death.

the city boy learned what it was like to spend time hunting, hiking, and fishing in the country. Babe loved it! He also loved going back to Baltimore for a visit as a successful baseball player. He had come a long way from the wild little boy he'd once been. When Babe showed his father the big check he'd received for being on the winning team in the World Series, Babe was thrilled at the look of pride and surprise in Big George's eyes.

The next season, 1917, was a memorable one for Babe, but not because he played well. On June 23, Babe found himself in the middle of one of the most famous arguments in the history of baseball. Babe had been chosen as the Red Sox starting pitcher against the Washington Senators. After warming up, he pitched to the first batter of the game.

"Ball one!" called umpire Brick Owens.

A ball! Babe thought that pitch had been a sure strike. He frowned and yelled a complaint toward the plate. Then he wound up and pitched the second pitch of the game.

"Ball two!" shouted the umpire.

Babe wondered if the umpire was losing his eyesight. He shouted again, and this time the umpire told him to be quiet. Babe closed his mouth and threw his third pitch.

"Ball three!" came the call.

Babe couldn't believe his ears. He walked around the mound, trying to calm himself down. Finally, with a terrible scowl on his face, he leaned over and threw his fourth pitch of the game.

"Ball four!"

It was the last straw. This time, Babe lost control of himself and ran toward the plate. Seconds later, the fight had gotten so bad, Babe was thrown out of the game. As he angrily stomped off the field, he heard Jack Barry, the new Boston manager, ordering Babe's old friend Ernie Shore to pitch for the Red Sox.

What happened after that is what made this game so famous. Ernie Shore went out onto the mound and *pitched a perfect game!* The player Babe walked was thrown out trying to steal second, and Shore got the next twenty-six batters out in a row, not letting a single man get on base. People still talk about Shore's brilliant pitching that day. Babe Ruth never stopped wondering what would have happened if he hadn't gotten himself thrown out of the game after throwing only four pitches.

After this bad experience, Babe settled down to pitch another great season for the Red Sox. The team didn't win the pennant that year, but Babe ended the season having once again won twenty-three games. Though he didn't know it at the time, it was the last season in which he would play only as a pitcher. In the years to come, Babe Ruth would finally be able to concentrate on his hitting.

The Babe Starts to Hit

As Babe became more famous as a ball player, his salary grew. He freely spent his money on cars, clothes, women friends, and rich food, but Babe was also very generous with his old friends. In particular, he never forgot Brother Matthias and the boys back at St. Mary's in Baltimore. He always sent large contributions to the school, and he visited whenever he could manage it. One of Babe's most prized possessions was a note he received from Brother Matthias. It said simply, "You're doing fine, George. I'm proud of you." It wasn't a long letter, but Babe treasured it throughout his life.

The year 1918 brought about a lot of changes in Babe's life. The United States had entered the First

World War in Europe, and the Red Sox manager, Jack Barry, enlisted in the army. Then the Red Sox owner, Harry Frazee, hired a man named Ed Barrow to be the new manager.

At this point in his career, Babe really wanted to change from being a pitcher to a hitter. But Manager Barrow was not too happy with the idea. Finally, he agreed to use Babe at first base in an exhibition game. Babe played so well that Barrow *had* to keep him in the line-up!

In May, Babe was in the line-up almost every day, either as a pitcher or an outfielder. But the extra effort of playing both fielder and pitcher was hard on him. Near the end of the month, he developed a terrible cold. He came to Boston's Fenway Park to play baseball anyway, but Barrow told him to go back to bed instead.

Babe felt so bad; he knew he had to obey the manager's order. But on the way home, one of the team trainers insisted on taking Babe to a drugstore. At the store the trainer bought some medicine called silver nitrate, which he used to paint the inside of Babe's throat. Silver nitrate was supposed to get rid of infection, but the medicine hurt his throat so much that Babe choked and then collapsed on the floor!

Within hours, people in Boston were worried stiff. "Have you heard the news?" they asked one another on the street. "Babe Ruth is dying!"

Fortunately, the rumors were false alarms. Babe was in the hospital for another week, but he quickly got better. When he appeared at Fenway Park the next week, the fans were on their feet, clapping and shouting his name. Babe would always blame his scratchy voice and later throat problems on the dose of silver nitrate he received that year.

When Babe returned to baseball after his illness, he played in the outfield and rarely went to the pitcher's mound. That's because Babe didn't want to pitch anymore. He was having serious disagreements with Ed Barrow because Barrow still wanted Babe to pitch. At one point, Babe became so angry, he left the ball club and said he wouldn't play for them anymore!

But late in July, the two men reached a compromise. Babe agreed to pitch *and* play outfield for the rest of the season. This was an extraordinary thing for a ball player to do. Pitching is one of the hardest jobs in baseball. Pitchers are usually given time off to rest between games. But not Babe. He pitched, played outfield, *and* batted fourth!

People were already talking about the way Babe

swung at the ball. His swing was unusual in several ways. For one thing, he used a heavier bat than most players did. For another, Babe held the bat at the very end, with his little finger curled around the tip. He held it so tightly and squeezed so hard, that he had calluses on his hand.

Baseball experts said Babe had patterned his swing on Shoeless Joe Jackson's of the Chicago White Sox. But what the fans noticed most was how much energy Babe put into his swing. He swung so hard, he turned almost completely around on his follow-through. And no matter what kind of pitch a pitcher would try to fool him with, Babe would eventually figure out a way to get a piece of it.

Babe later said if he missed a ball the first time a pitcher threw it, he would have figured out a way of hitting it the next time. Even Babe himself didn't have a clear idea how he was able to connect so often. Years later, he said that he thought he must have had a way of sensing what to do with the bat.

By August, Babe was leading the team in hitting *and* pitching. It seemed there was nothing Babe Ruth couldn't do. But then his baseball playing was sadly interrupted. The news came from Baltimore that Babe's father had died in a tragic accident.

As soon as they could, Babe and Helen took the

train to Baltimore to attend Big George's funeral. It was a difficult time for Babe. His mother had died when he was a student at St. Mary's, and he rarely saw his eighteen-year-old sister, Mamie. The Ruth family may not have been a close one, and George Ruth may not have been a perfect father, but Babe felt great sadness now that both of his parents were gone.

A New Record

A saddened Babe returned to Boston to play out the rest of the 1918 season. Thanks to his extraordinary efforts, the Red Sox won the pennant and went on to win the World Series four games to two. It was in this series that Babe extended his streak of scoreless innings pitched in the World Series to twenty-nine—a record that stood for forty-two years!

Things were now going beautifully for Babe in baseball, but he and Helen were having personal problems. Babe always loved leading the "good life," and this life sometimes included staying out late at night. As the Babe became more famous, he spent more time away from home. Helen became lonely and frustrated at being all by herself on the farm she and Babe owned in Sudbury, Massachusetts. While Babe was living it up in town or on the road, she was becoming unhappy.

But baseball fans across the country cared only about Babe's amazing baseball ability, and Babe was well on his way to becoming a national superstar. It seemed as if everyone, everywhere, knew who he was.

Babe's growing fame may have been the reason that the 1919 season got off to a rocky start. Babe was not happy about the terms of his contract, and for a while, it looked as if Ruth would be a "hold-out"—a player who won't play until he gets the terms he wants. Babe was great, and he knew it. But he'd never been able to stay away from baseball for very long. By April he was ready to join the rest of the team in Florida for spring training.

In spring training, Babe hit so well that it looked as if he would have one of his best seasons ever. In April, he began knocking out home runs and it looked as though he might set a record! The American League record for home runs at the time was sixteen, by "Socks" Seybold of the 1902 Athletics. The recognized major league record was twenty-five, by Buck Freeman of the 1899 Washington League club.

When Babe passed the twenty-five home run mark, however, someone dug up a twenty-seven home run record, hit by Ned Williamson of the White Sox in 1884. But Babe wasn't discouraged. He knew he could break *any* record. On September 20, 1919, he hit another home run, tying Williamson's mark, and baseball fans across the nation went wild.

Still, Babe did have a few problems with the team *off* the field. Early in the season, he got into a tangle with Manager Barrow. As usual, Babe couldn't see any good reasons for following the rules Ed Barrow had set up for his players' behavior. One of those rules was a strict team curfew that stated at what time all the players had to be in the hotel for the night.

Whenever the team was on the road, Barrow stayed up until everyone had returned to the hotel. One night, well past the team's curfew, Babe snuck into his room. He thought he had escaped Barrow's notice. But then he heard a loud knock on the door. The manager burst into the room and found Babe lying in bed, smoking his pipe.

When Ed Barrow discovered that Babe was fully

dressed under the covers, he gave the ball player a good chewing out. At first, Babe was embarrassed and apologetic. But by the next day his embarrassment had turned to anger. He was the great Babe Ruth, he thought to himself, and no one in the world had the right to speak to him that way!

In the clubhouse before the game, Babe stomped up to Barrow and insulted him. Barrow lost his temper—and then he announced the bad news. Babe was suspended from the team!

At first, Babe couldn't believe what he was hearing; but when he realized the manager was serious, he began to feel terrible. As usual, he had acted without thinking first, and this time he had gone too far. Soon after the argument, he went to Barrow and apologized. He promised to be on his best behavior in the future, and the two men shook hands on the agreement.

As the baseball season neared its end, the whole nation was watching the Red Sox to see if Babe Ruth would set a new home run record. The Babe didn't disappoint them. In late September, at the Polo Grounds in New York, he hit his twenty-eighth home run, passing Williamson's mark. A few days later, in Washington, he hit his twenty-ninth.

The whole country was excited. And even though

the Red Sox didn't win the pennant that year, it didn't matter very much to the Boston fans. They were thrilled by Babe Ruth's performance and proud that he wore a Red Sox uniform. They might not have been so happy, however, if they had known what was going to happen in 1920—1919 was Babe Ruth's last season with the Boston Red Sox.

Welcome to the Big Apple

Today, many people think Babe Ruth was a Yankee for his entire career. They hardly remember his years as a Red Sox or the year 1920 Red Sox owner Harry Frazee sold Babe to the New York Yankees. Though the financial arrangements were very complicated, people in Boston were stunned to learn that the Yankee owners, Colonel Ruppert and Colonel Huston had paid about $125,000 for Babe. At the time, that amount was the most money ever paid for a single ball player.

"How could this have happened?" the Red Sox fans asked each other. Why would anyone want to sell the great Babe Ruth, especially the year after he had just set a new home run record? In Boston, people felt the "heart" had been taken out of base-ball.

Obviously, in New York, people felt differently. They gave Babe Ruth a warm welcome. In many ways, it seemed as if New York City was *made* for Babe. It was a big, exciting, noisy, unpredictable city, and Babe Ruth was a big, exciting, noisy, un-predictable person.

In 1920, fans were ready to be excited about base-ball again. World War I was over, and Americans could relax and enjoy sports once again. A new, "livelier" baseball was introduced to the game. When it was hit, it traveled farther than the older ball had. And Babe Ruth had come to New York!

Unfortunately, after all the excitement about the trade, Babe got off to a bad start. During spring training a fan shouted so many insults from the bleachers that Babe lost his temper and jumped into the stands. Imagine Babe's surprise when, as he chased the fan, the man whirled around and pulled out a knife! Before the fight could get too serious, another player pulled Babe away from the man and hurried him back down onto the field. Then, in April, Babe had some injuries, and he just couldn't get on the right track with his hitting. Early in the season, fans had jammed the ballpark, hoping to see Babe hit a home run. But now, the Yankee fans began to get impatient. If New York had spent all that money to get the Babe, why wasn't he playing well? Why was he striking out and getting hurt all the time? Why were they reading such headlines in the newspapers as, "The Babe Fizzles in the Pinch"?

Luckily, by the middle of May, Babe started hitting. He was ahead of the record-setting pace he had set the year before, and the fans were his friends again. They poured into the Polo Grounds, setting new attendance records with every game. People who couldn't fit into the ballpark stood across the way where they could see the scoreboard and listen to the roar of the crowd.

Babe was hitting home runs at an incredible pace. He hit twelve homers by the end of May, and twelve more in June. Soon he was hitting a home run in practically every game. Sportswriters tried to outdo each other, coming up with nicknames for the Babe, such as the Sultan of Swat, the Caliph of Clout, and the Mastodonic Mauler. He was also called the *Bambino,* which is the Italian word for babe. Sometimes the headlines in the paper would say only, "Bam Hits One." No one had to ask who "bam" was. By July 15 he had tied his 1919 record of twenty-nine home runs, and he finished the year with fifty-four.

In addition to setting home run records, Babe was also hitting the ball *farther* than anyone else ever had. Before long, because of Ruth's powerful shots, the foul lines, which used to go only to the end of the outfield, had to be extended up into the seats and all the way to the roof!

Soon it seemed as if it were almost impossible to get Babe Ruth out. The pitchers for the opposing teams didn't know *what* to do! No matter what kind of ball they threw, the Babe smacked it. After a while, the pitchers and their managers came up with a plan. If they couldn't strike Babe out with their pitching, they would walk him on purpose to keep him from hitting a home run. It wasn't a bad idea, but many spectators didn't like it. People were so eager to see the Bambino hit a home run, that even the fans from the *opposing* teams booed when Ruth was walked on purpose. Today Babe Ruth still holds the record for the most bases on balls, or walks, ever received.

People had never seen home run hitting like Babe's. Years later, when Babe talked about the reaction of the 1920's fans to his record-breaking 54 home runs, he compared it to the way people today might feel about a player's hitting 200. It seemed just that amazing.

Babe's personal life in New York City was also amazing. He and Helen had moved into the Ansonia Hotel in Manhattan, and the Babe was living it up, spending a lot of money. He loved to go out at night—often without his wife—and he frequently went to parties with a lot of famous people.

People told stories about Babe Ruth's personal life—about his drinking, driving fancy cars, and being around beautiful women. But most of their stories still had to do with baseball. Nothing seemed so incredible as Babe's first year as a Yankee. He finished the season with a batting average of .376, with thirty-six doubles and nine triples in addition to his home runs.

Unfortunately for baseball, the Babe's hitting was not enough to make up for two terrible things that happened that year. Firstly, in a tragic accident, a player named Ray Chapman was killed when a pitched ball hit him in the head while he was up at bat. And secondly, 1920 was the year it was discovered that the World Series of 1919, between the Chicago White Sox and the Cincinnati Reds, had been "fixed"—that is, eight Chicago players had been paid to *lose* the World Series on purpose.

When the public heard about the scandal, soon to be known as the Black Sox scandal, people felt sick. Baseball was more than a sport to many people. They looked up to baseball players as the nation's heroes. When the public learned that eight players, including the famous Shoeless Joe Jackson, had been so dishonest, they wondered if they could ever believe in baseball again. A famous story from this time tells of a little boy who recognized Joe Jackson on a Chicago street. With tears in his eyes, the boy went up to the ball player and said, "Say it ain't so, Joe!" The story shows how betrayed the American public felt.

After the scandal, a baseball commissioner, Judge Kennesaw Mountain Landis, was appointed. His job was to work hard to make sure such a scandal never happened again. He punished the eight men who were involved and helped bring back some of the people's faith in baseball. Babe Ruth's amazing new home run record also gave the fans something positive to think about that year.

"If my home run hitting in 1920 established a new era in baseball," Babe said, "helped the fans of the nation, young and old, forget the past and the terrible fact that they had been 'sold out,' that's all the epitaph I want."

After 1920, no one expected Ruth to be able to do any better than he already had. But early in the 1921 season, he immediately began hitting home runs at the same amazing pace he'd shown the year before. Once again, all the nation's fans were watching New York to see if Babe could break his own record of fifty-four home runs in one season. And that's just what Babe did! On September 15, Babe hit his fifty-fifth home run. In the games that followed, he hit four more to establish a *new* home run record of fifty-nine! And, to make things more exciting, he helped the Yankees win their first pennant!

The 1921 World Series was an exciting one for New Yorkers because it placed two New York teams, the Yankees and the Giants, against each other. Babe was eager to play, but he had hurt his arm in the first game. The fans were worried that he wouldn't be able to play after that, but to everyone's amazement, he played in the second game—with his arm in a bandage! The crowd cheered wildly when they saw him playing with an injury.

In spite of Babe's heroics, the Giants won the Series. Even so, it had been another incredible year for Babe. He'd not only broken his own home run record, he'd batted an amazing .378.

People who follow baseball records and figures claim that Babe's statistics in 1920 and 1921 are the most impressive they've ever seen.

The House That Ruth Built

By 1922, Babe was earning more money than he'd ever dreamed possible, and he was spending it almost as fast as he was earning it. One of Babe's favorite purchases was his car. It was a long, low, fire-engine-red Packard roadster. He didn't always drive it as carefully as he should, but whenever he was stopped by a policeman, the officer would be so thrilled to meet the famous ball player, he usually let Babe off with a warning.

Babe enjoyed his fame and fortune but it wasn't always fun. He had so many fans now, he and Helen had almost no privacy at all. When he came home, he often found total strangers on his doorstep, waiting to talk to him or just to catch a glimpse of him!

Eventually, he started sneaking in through the janitor's entrance so he could get into his own apartment without having to talk to anyone.

At this time, Babe had the good fortune to meet a man named Christy Walsh. He offered to manage Babe's finances for him. After that, although Babe still spent a lot of money, he never had to worry about money problems again.

Babe and Christy Walsh put Babe's complicated financial affairs in order, but the next year, 1922, was not a good one for Babe Ruth. By now he was the highest paid player in baseball, earning $52,000 a year. The Yankee owners offered him $50,000, but Babe said he had always wanted to earn $1,000 a week so he asked for $52,000! Some people criticized Babe for asking for so much money, but he felt he was worth it. A man can be a baseball player for only a short part of his life, he explained. He has to earn money while he can.

Despite his high salary, Babe didn't hit very well at the beginning of the 1922 season. The fans didn't like this, and they began booing him. In May, Babe got angry at an umpire and threw dirt in the man's face. When Babe was thrown out of the game, a fan shouted an insult, and Babe jumped into the stands to chase him. Babe was suspended for one game and fined. He also lost his job as captain of the Yankees.

As the season went on, things didn't get much better. Babe's home run hitting dropped from fifty-nine to thirty-five, and he missed playing in forty-four games. He batted only .118 in the World Series against the Giants. He gained weight and let himself get out of shape. He was involved in more fights and was suspended from the team several times.

To make matters worse, in September some reporters in New York learned that Babe and Helen had a child. But the baby hadn't just been born—it was a sixteen-month-old toddler! The newspapers reported all about it. "Ruth a Daddy for Sixteen Months and Has Hidden Facts from World," one headline read.

Naturally, people were curious about the baby. In Cleveland, Ohio, where the Yankees were playing, Babe was asked about it. He claimed that the baby, named Dorothy, had been born on February 2, 1921 in Presbyterian Hospital. She had been in an incubator for much of her early life, he said, and after that had been cared for by a nurse. Now, however, she was a healthy little girl.

Meanwhile, back in New York, Helen told newspaper reporters that the baby had been born on

June 7, in St. Vincent's Hospital! The reporters tried to investigate the two different stories, but they never found an answer. Some people asked Helen if Dorothy had been adopted. She became angry and insisted the baby was hers. Some people said that, while Babe might be Dorothy's father, another woman—not Helen—might really be her mother. In 1988, Dorothy Ruth Pirone wrote a book called *My Dad The Babe*, in which she said that Helen was not her real mother.

With all the controversy now surrounding Babe's playing and his personal life, 1922 proved to be a difficult season for him. But he felt even worse a few weeks after the season ended. Some sportswriters got together and organized a dinner in the Babe's honor; but when he got there, everyone took turns standing up and making fun of him. The most painful remarks came from New York's state senator, James Walker, who would one day become mayor of New York City. Walker knew how much Babe Ruth cared about the children who admired him. In his speech, he accused Babe of letting down all the fans, especially the "dirty-faced kids" of America.

After this speech, Babe felt so terrible he was too choked up to speak. When he could finally talk, he said, "I know as well as anybody else just what mistakes I made last season. There's no use in me trying to get away from them.

"But let me tell you something. . . . Tomorrow I'm going to my farm. I'm going to work my head off—and maybe part of my stomach!"

True to his word, Babe, Helen, and Dorothy headed for their farm in Sudbury, Massachusetts. Babe spent the fall and winter hunting, fishing, riding horses, and chopping wood. He lost weight and started to get himself back into top shape.

Meanwhile, back in New York, a major construction project was under way. Up until 1920, the Yankees had shared space with the New York Giants in the stadium called the Polo Grounds. But that year, mainly because of Babe Ruth's performance, 350,000 more fans came to see the Yankees than the Giants. The Giants, who owned the Polo Grounds, didn't like this and asked the Yankees to find another place to play.

In 1922, on a piece of land in the Bronx, construction began on a new ballpark. Within a year, a beautiful two-million-dollar stadium had been completed. Though many people wanted to call it Ruth Field, it was named Yankee Stadium. Part of the stadium, the bleachers in right field, was nicknamed Ruthville. This is where Babe hit so many of his home runs.

On April 18, 1923, the Yankees played their first game in Yankee Stadium. Though the stadium was only supposed to hold 65,000 people, 75,000 had been crowded inside. This time, Babe didn't let his fans down. He had gotten his weight down to 215 pounds, and he was determined to concentrate on playing ball and nothing else. In the fourth inning, he hit a home run with two men on base. The fans went wild. The Yankees went on to win the game 4–1.

By this time, there was a saying about the Yankees: "As Ruth goes, so go the Yankees." It meant that if Babe played poorly, so would the whole team and if Babe played well, the rest of the team would also play well. In 1923, this was definitely the case. Babe hit only forty-one home runs, but his batting average was .393. He got along with everyone on the team, including manager Miller Huggins, and he won the American League's Most Valuable Player award. Babe played well and so did the Yankees. They finally beat the Giants to win the 1923 World Series.

In 1924, Lou Gehrig, another great ball player, joined the Yankees. Babe had a great year, even though the Yankees didn't win the pennant. A professor at Columbia University was so impressed with Babe's athletic ability, he gave him a series of tests in hearing, vision, and coordination to find out what made him such a good ball player. At the end of the tests the professor concluded that Babe's abilities were extraordinary. In other words, he said, Babe was "one out of a million."

Babe himself never completely understood what made him such a good player. Years later, he talked about how he'd never been very smart in school. But his intuition for baseball, he agreed, was another matter.

Babe had such a good year in 1924, it was hard to believe that 1925 could be so bad. For one thing, Babe and Helen's marriage was now in serious trouble. Babe was often seen out on the town with other women. At one point, Babe and Helen separated. They got back together, but they were still not very happy. At this time, Babe started to go out with Claire Merritt Hodgson. Unlike his attitude toward the other women he had been seen with, Babe's feelings for Claire were serious. Naturally, Helen was lonely and unhappy about this, but she and Babe wouldn't consider a divorce.

Babe had as many problems in baseball as he had

at home. His hitting dropped off again, and he was not getting along with the Yankee manager, Miller Huggins. This was also the year of Babe's most famous stomachache.

After spring training in Florida, Babe was already feeling slightly sick when the team left St. Petersburg, but he kept on eating anyway—especially hot dogs. Later, in Asheville, North Carolina, he developed a fever and collapsed. He was put on a train for New York, but by the time the train arrived in Manhattan, he was almost unconscious. An ambulance arrived, and Babe was rushed to the hospital.

Once again, the news hit the papers quickly. Headlines reported that Babe was dying or dead. It turned out that he had an infection in his intestines. Doctors performed surgery, and Babe stayed in the hospital for a little less than two months. He laughed at a notice of his death that had been printed in a newspaper from England. Once he was well again, the newspapers called Babe's illness "The Stomachache Heard Round the World."

Babe never really pulled himself together again during the 1925 season, and some of his critics said he might be all washed up in baseball. But the next year was another story. During the winter before the 1926 season, Babe's financial manager, Christy Walsh, took Babe to Artie McGovern's gym in New York to begin a work-out program. Babe had to ride bikes, do leg exercises, and play catch with a heavy ball called a "medicine ball." It was hard, painful work, but by February Babe described himself as "hard as nails."

Being in such good shape paid off. In the 1926 season, Babe hit 47 homers and drove in 155 runs. The Yankees won the pennant and got ready to play in the World Series against the St. Louis Cardinals. It was from this World Series that a famous Babe Ruth story came.

Johnny Sylvester was an eleven-year-old boy who had been badly hurt in a fall in New Jersey. His doctors weren't sure if Johnny would live. To help cheer up his son, Johnny's father called Yankee Stadium and asked for an autographed picture of Babe Ruth.

Somehow, Babe heard about the call and decided to visit Johnny in person. He drove to the hospital in New Jersey and spent some time with the sick boy. When he left, he promised to hit a home run in the World Series for Johnny.

The World Series started the next day. But it wasn't until the fourth game that Babe Ruth had the chance to keep his promise.

In the first inning, Babe hit a home run off the first pitch he received in the game. In the third inning, he hit a *second* home run. Then, in the sixth inning, he hit *another* home run. This one flew so far, it went all the way out of the St. Louis stadium! For the first time in history, someone had hit three home runs in one World Series game! No one knows for sure which home run was for Johnny Sylvester, but Johnny recovered from his injuries and went on to lead a long life. Johnny was lucky, but unfortunately for the Yankees, the Cardinals went on to win the 1926 World Series.

By the end of the year, Babe and Helen had separated from each other for good. They sold their farm and didn't try to live with one another again. Babe still spent a lot of time with Claire Hodgson, but he also went out with many other women.

Babe Ruth was playing well again, but it was the 1927 Yankees that topped all. Throughout his life, Babe always referred to the 1927 team as the greatest in history, and today sportscasters still compare modern teams to the '27 Yankees. They set a standard that has never been forgotten.

That year almost every single player on the Yankees played like a star. The batters smacked out an incredible number of hits, but the pitchers were outstanding as well. One of the best pitchers the Yankees bought that season was an Oklahoma farmer named Wilcy Moore.

No one knew much about Wilcy when he came to the team, but they soon learned that he was a solid, reliable relief pitcher. Babe became friends with Wilcy, and, as usual, he enjoyed teasing Wilcy and giving him a hard time.

Like most pitchers, Wilcy didn't hit very well. During spring training, Babe bet the pitcher three hundred dollars that he wouldn't get three hits all season. Wilcy accepted the bet—and then got five hits! Babe paid up, and Wilcy used the money to buy two new mules for his farm back home. He named one of them Babe and the other one Ruth!

One of the most exciting things about the 1927 season was the home run race between Babe Ruth and Lou Gehrig. Beginning in April, Babe and Lou each started hitting homers, one after the other, in game after game. By early August, Lou was ahead of Babe, thirty-eight to thirty-five, and the fans were wondering if Ruth had finally met his match.

Then, as August continued, Lou's pace slowed down while Babe's exploded. He hit so many home runs, people said he might break his own record of fifty-nine. There weren't very many games left—could Babe do it?

When Babe hit his fifty-sixth home run, the fans were so excited, they wanted just to touch him—or his uniform, or his bat. They particularly wanted to get hold of his bat. Babe Ruth's bat would be the souvenir of a lifetime! After one home run, Babe carried his bat around the bases with him so none of the fans could get it. Even so, a boy jumped out of the stands and tried to snatch the bat. Babe picked him up and crossed home plate with the bat *and* the boy under his arm!

After home run number fifty-six, Babe didn't hit another for two games. The sportswriters said he couldn't possibly set a new record. There were only four games left! But in the first of the last four games, Babe hit number fifty-seven—a grand slam home run. In the next game, he hit *two* homers, numbers fifty-eight and fifty-nine. And then, on September 30, he did it. He stepped to the plate and belted out number sixty! Though the pitcher argued that the ball was foul, the umpire declared it fair, and the new record was set. After the game, Babe jumped up and down, hugging his teammates and shouting, "Sixty, count 'em, sixty!"

*   *   *

Over the years, Babe became close friends with Lou Gehrig. He, Lou, and some other teammates would often travel up to Lou's home in New Rochelle for a visit after a game. "Mom Gehrig" was a wonderful cook, and Babe loved to eat huge servings of her famous pigs knuckles. He was so grateful for the home-cooked meals, he gave her a little Chihuahua dog for a present. In turn, she named the dog "Jidge," which was one of Babe's nicknames.

The year 1929 was a year of change for Babe. In January Helen Ruth was killed in a fire in Watertown, Massachusetts.

Though Babe and Helen had been separated for some time, Babe was still very upset about Helen's death. During a press conference a few days after her death, he broke down in tears and said he still loved her.

In the book she later wrote, Dorothy stated that no one told her about her mother's death for a number of days. She described how she was taken out of school and sent to live with a woman named Miss Dooley in Brooklyn. It was Miss Dooley who finally told Dorothy that her mother was dead.

Three months later, Babe and Claire Hodgson were married. A few months after that, Dorothy came to live with Babe and Claire as well as Julia—Claire's daughter from her first marriage—in their apartment on Riverside Drive in New York City. After the marriage, Claire decided to help Babe control some of his bad habits, such as over-eating, over-drinking, and over-spending. Changing Babe completely would be impossible, but Claire did her best.

Although his personal life was changing for the better, Babe's life on the baseball field was not. The Yankees weren't even in the running for the pennant that year. And, in September, to the shock of all the players, Yankee manager Miller Huggins died. Babe cried in the clubhouse with the rest of his teammates. It was a sad time for all of them. Miller Huggins' death gave Babe an idea. For some time, Babe had been thinking about being a manager. Near the end of the season, he went to Yankee owner Colonel Jacob Ruppert and said he would like a chance to manage the team.

The Colonel answered Babe sharply. He said Babe couldn't even manage his *own* life—how could he expect to manage others? This was not the last time Babe would try to become a manager. And it was not the last time he would hear a response like this.

The 1930s

"Who do you think you are, Babe Ruth?" In 1930, this was a common expression in America. It meant, "Do you think you're so wonderful you can do *anything?*" By this time in his career, Babe Ruth was a living legend. His name was a household word. People challenged one another to see who could come up with a better Babe Ruth story. They didn't just talk about his baseball playing, either. They talked about his convertible car, his raccoon coat, his drinking, and his relationships with women. They also talked about his eating habits. One story said Babe once ate an omelet made of eighteen eggs—along with three slices of ham and half a loaf of bread! Another story said

Babe ate at least three hot dogs during every single baseball game!

One of the most famous Babe Ruth stories is about his enormous salary. In 1930, Babe signed a contract for an incredible $80,000 a year. Yankee owner Colonel Ruppert told him he was now getting paid more money than Herbert Hoover, the president of the United States.

"Why not?" Babe answered with his large grin. "I had a better year than he did!"

Babe was now a world-famous, wealthy man. But he hadn't forgotten his roots. He still sent money back to St. Mary's school. Once, when some of the buildings at St. Mary's burned down, Babe took the school band with him on a barnstorming trip out west. On the trip, Babe and other well-known baseball players played in games for local crowds from town to town while the St. Mary's band played the music. With the money people paid to see these games, Babe helped the school replace their burned buildings.

Whenever he had the time, Babe visited children's wards in hospitals. Some newspaper writers accused him of doing this only for publicity. But Lefty Gomez, a teammate of the Babe's, disagreed with those writers. Gomez wrote that Babe visited all those hospitals because of his love for children. He said that Babe didn't even want the press to know what he was doing. Babe went to the hospitals just to make the sick children happy.

One sportswriter told a story about driving sixty miles with Babe one day to visit a sick child before a World Series game in Chicago. Babe told the writer not to write anything about the visit later or he would "let him have it."

Babe was still playing baseball, but he was getting older. In 1932, he was thirty-eight years old and having some trouble with his legs. He was still hitting well, but other, younger players, like Jimmie Foxx and Lou Gehrig, were hitting better. Right before the World Series, Babe got sick, and many people thought he wouldn't even be able to play in the Series at all.

But Babe recovered in time for the Series, which became the scene for the most famous Babe Ruth story of all time. It took place in Chicago, in the third game of the Series, but it had really begun earlier. For some reason, there was bad feeling between the Cubs and the Yankees. Every time their teams played, there was a lot of shouting back and forth between the players.

By the time the Yankees arrived in Chicago for the third game of the Series, feelings were running hot. The Yankees had already won the first two games in New York, and the Chicago fans were not happy. The Cub players weren't happy, either; and when Babe stepped up to the plate in the fifth inning with the score tied 4–4, they let him know about it. They started yelling insults about his age and weight.

"My ears had been blistered so much before in my baseball career," Babe said, "that I thought they had lost all feeling. But the blast that was turned on me by the Cub players and some of the fans penetrated and cut deep. Some of the fans started throwing vegetables and fruit at me!"

Babe stepped back out of the batter's box to collect his wits. Then he stepped back in. Charlie Root, the pitcher, hurled his first pitch, and Babe let it pass. Before the umpire could say a word, Babe raised his hand, held up one finger and shouted, "Strike one!"

The Cubs got noisier and more insulting, and Root threw his second pitch. Again, Babe didn't swing. Instead, he held up his right hand and yelled, "Strike two!"

When the count was two balls and two strikes, the

fans and the Cub players went wild, yelling and taunting the Babe. But Babe just grinned at them. The story goes that as Root got ready to throw his next pitch, Babe pointed to the bleachers deep in center field. The crowd jumped to its feet, jeering and shouting.

Babe later wrote a description of what happened next. He said Root threw a fast ball that definitely would have been a strike if Babe had let it pass. But Babe knew that this was *the* pitch. He smacked it with everything he had, and it felt terrific. That hit was the longest home run ever hit at Wrigley Field! It flew over the center fielder's head and landed in the stands, exactly in the spot where Babe had pointed.

As Babe ran around the bases, he laughed out loud. Some of the players heard him calling himself a lucky bum.

Later, Babe described this home run as the "funniest, proudest moment" he'd ever had in baseball. A newspaper headline the next day read: RUTH CALLS HIS SHOT. Baseball fans could talk about nothing else.

Over the years, people have argued about whether this famous "called shot" ever really happened. Some, including the pitcher, Charlie Root, say it didn't. They say Babe was just waving his hand, or reaching up to scratch his nose. They say it is just a story created by sportswriters and enthusiastic fans. But there is a lot of evidence to show that Babe Ruth really was capable of predicting where his home runs would land and that he was often able to choose his exact moment when he would hit them. Whether or not it actually happened, this event was in the 1948 movie called *The Babe Ruth Story*, and it is now a permanent part of the great Babe Ruth legend.

Babe always said he would retire in 1933, after his twentieth season. But at the end of that year, he decided to keep on playing. One reason was that Babe hated to give up playing the game he loved. In addition, he still wanted an opportunity to manage a team, particularly the Yankees. He hoped that if he stayed active as a player, his chances at a managing job might be better.

At the end of the 1934 season, Babe and a number of other players went on a barnstorming trip to Japan. They had a wonderful reception there. Great crowds of people came to see them. Babe was the star player for the Japanese fans.

After Japan, Babe and Claire visited several other

countries, including France and England. When they returned to America, in February of 1935, Babe received an offer to play for the Boston Braves. He really wanted to stay in New York and manage the Yankees, but he realized that this was probably not going to happen. The Yankees released him from their team, and Babe headed for Boston.

But playing for the Braves didn't work out very well. Babe thought he would be a player *and* an "assistant manager." But once he arrived in Boston, he found that he wouldn't have much chance to help manage. The main reason the Braves wanted Babe was for publicity and his ability to draw big crowds. But Babe wasn't hitting very well, and the Boston fans booed him. Both he and the Braves were disappointed with each other.

Even so, Babe did have one shining moment with Boston. On May 25, the Braves played the Pittsburgh Pirates. In the first inning, Babe hit a two-run homer. In the third inning, he hit another two-run homer. Then, in the seventh inning, Babe cracked out his third home run of the day!

"I never saw a ball hit so hard before or since," one of the Pirates' pitchers said. "He was fat and old, but he still had that great swing. Even when he missed, you could hear the bat go swish."

In spite of Babe's great hitting, the Braves went on to lose that game to the Pirates. But the three home runs were very important. They were the 712th, 713th, and 714th home runs of Babe Ruth's career. Babe's 714 career home run record would hold for thirty-nine years. It was finally broken by Hank Aaron in 1974.

On May 28, Babe played again in a game against the Cincinnati Reds. He had a lot of trouble handling his position in center field, and the fans were giving him a hard time. At last, a saddened, discouraged Babe took himself out of the game.

The famous sportscaster Red Barber wrote a description of what happened next. He said the fans hissed and booed while the Babe looked angry and sad. As Babe left the field, a little boy ran up to him and grabbed his knees. Babe picked him up and hugged him.

"That went down in my book as a home run, Babe's 715th," Barber wrote. "The fans saw it that way, too. They hushed immediately." Two days later, Babe played in his last game ever in major league baseball.

Life After Baseball

Babe Ruth's whole life had been baseball, and he wanted nothing more than to stay in the game, somehow. He wanted to manage a team, but in 1935, he simply couldn't find a job. One reason was that none of the major league managers were ready to quit at that time, and there just weren't any openings. But another more important reason was that baseball owners wondered if Babe could do a good job managing a team. Babe had earned a lot of money as a player. Would he expect to be paid a lot of money as a manager? they asked. He had always had a reputation for being difficult. Would he be able to get along with his players?

Whatever the reasons, a management job never

opened up for Babe. He felt disappointed and let down by the sport for which he'd done so much. A newspaper cartoon from this year shows that some people agreed with him. It showed a picture of a tired old Babe, dressed in rags, walking down the road away from Yankee Stadium. Following Babe was a pack of vicious dogs trying to bite him. One dog was labeled "ungrateful owners." Another was labeled "jeering fans." A large sign on Yankee Stadium read, "The House That Ruth Built."

Even though Babe was disappointed with the way people in baseball were treating him, he didn't spend his time sitting around feeling sorry for himself. He often went out to the country, where he hunted, fished, boated, and drove around in one of his famous cars.

During his retirement, Babe played golf. He loved the game, and soon was spending as much time as he could out on the golf course. He wasn't a bad player, and he often won small prizes in tournaments. Babe also traveled around the world, made his picks for each year's all-star teams, and played in exhibition baseball games—just for fun. And, as always, he kept up his visits to the children's wards of hospitals.

In 1939, Babe attended the opening of the Baseball Hall of Fame in Cooperstown, New York. When he gave his speech, he talked about the importance of little children learning how to play baseball.

The year 1939 was a good one for baseball because the Hall of Fame opened. But it was a sad year, too. This was the year that Lou Gehrig, the great "Iron Man" was forced to leave baseball. Lou hadn't had his usual good season in 1938, and he'd begun to suspect something was physically wrong with him. His poor play continued; and on May 2, 1939, he decided he shouldn't play for a while.

This was a terrible shock for America. Lou hadn't missed a game since he started playing as a regular back in 1925! Baseball fans feared that only something very serious could keep Lou out of the game, and they soon learned they were right. Lou was desperately ill with a muscular disease that would one day be known as "Lou Gehrig's Disease." The Iron Man did not have long to live. On July 4, Lou Gehrig Day was held in Yankee Stadium to honor the famous ball player.

Though they had once been close friends, Lou and Babe had argued sometime before this and hadn't spoken to each other in several years. But when Babe joined the audience on Lou Gehrig Day, he could only remember the good times he had shared with his old teammate. As he listened to Lou's speech, he sat in his seat and cried.

The speech, though short, has become famous in baseball history. ". . . They say I've had a bad break," Lou said into the microphone, "but I have an awful lot to live for. With all this, I consider myself the luckiest man on the face of the earth."

As Lou started off the field, Babe couldn't help himself. With tears in his eyes, he hurried up to Lou, put his arm around him, and gave him a hug. For the next two years, until Lou died, Babe often visited his old friend in the hospital.

After Lou died in 1941, Babe was asked to play the part of himself in a movie about Lou Gehrig, called *Pride of the Yankees.* He went to Hollywood in 1942 and worked hard on the film. After catching pneumonia, he went back to his family in New York. There, he played golf, listened to the radio shows that were popular at that time, and spent time with his grandchildren. In her book about her father, Dorothy wrote that Babe took great pride in her children. He loved to make faces for them and bounce them around on his lap.

During this time, the United States became involved in World War II. Babe worked for the Red Cross and played golf games to help raise money for the war effort. He also went to California to help with the filming of *The Babe Ruth Story*, a movie being made about his life.

From time to time, Babe also played in an exhibition baseball game. Whenever he did, he felt like a new person—excited, strong, and young again. He still loved putting on a uniform, getting out on the field, and swinging a bat. Although nothing ever did work out, Babe always hoped that a major league job would come his way.

At the end of 1946, Babe developed a terrible pain over his left eye. He entered a hospital in New York, where he had an operation on a cancerous growth in his neck. Most of the cancer was removed, but not all of it could be. Babe never completely recovered his health.

April 27, 1947 was declared "Babe Ruth Day" at Yankee Stadium by baseball commissioner A. B. "Happy" Chandler. Though Babe had been out of baseball for years, 60,000 people crowded the stadium to honor the most famous player in history. Babe's fans were shocked when they saw his appearance. They remembered him as tall, strong, and bigger than life. The man they saw was thin and so weak he had trouble walking out onto the field.

Even though he was physically weak, what Babe said was full of power. He hadn't brought a written speech along with him, but instead, spoke right from his heart. His voice was hoarse, and he spoke in a whisper, but the stadium was so quiet, no one missed a word.

Babe said that the only real game in the world was baseball and that children had to be given a chance to play when they were as young as six or seven years old. If they had that chance, and they tried hard enough, Babe said, they'd be bound to come out on top.

"There've been so many lovely things said about me," Babe finished, "I'm glad I had the opportunity to thank everybody. Thank you."

Babe's health improved for a short time in 1947, and he was able to do some traveling, attend a few baseball games, and write his autobiography with Bob Considine. He also started The Babe Ruth Foundation, an organization to help underprivileged children.

Unfortunately, Babe's good health didn't last. In June of 1948 he made his last appearance in Yankee Stadium, in his old uniform, as baseball fans and colleagues honored him. Shortly afterward he entered Memorial Hospital in Manhattan. Babe stayed in the hospital for two months. During that time, he had many visitors, including the little boy, Johnny Sylvester, for whom he'd hit a home run back in 1926.

On August 16, Babe Ruth died of cancer. Americans everywhere were saddened by the news. President Harry Truman said the country would mourn Babe's passing. Former President Hoover told his favorite Babe Ruth story: A small boy once asked the president for three autographs, so that he could trade *two* of them for *one* of Babe Ruth's!

Babe's body was brought to Yankee Stadium, where more than 100,000 people came to say their last good-byes. Later, during the funeral service at St. Patrick's Cathedral in New York City, more than 100,000 people lined the streets in the pouring rain, hoping for a chance to say good-bye to the Bambino.

Babe was buried in the town of Valhalla, New York, where people still stop by, almost every day, to pay their respects at the grave of one of America's greatest legends.

Highlights in the Life of
BABE RUTH

1895 George Herman Ruth, Jr., is born in Baltimore, Maryland, on February 6.

1902 George is sent to St. Mary's Industrial School for Boys outside Baltimore.

1914 George leaves St. Mary's to join the minor league Baltimore Orioles. He travels with the Orioles to spring training, where the other players nickname him *Babe.*

In July, Babe joins a major league team, the Boston Red Sox.

In October, he marries Helen Woodford.

1916 Babe wins twenty-three games for the Red Sox. He pitches and wins the longest game in World Series history.

1917 Babe again wins twenty-three games for the Red Sox.

1918 Babe begins playing outfield so he can have more opportunities to hit.

1919 Babe hits twenty-nine home runs, setting a new home-run record.

1920 Babe joins the New York Yankees. In his first season there, he sets a new home-run record of fifty-four.

1921 Babe breaks his own home-run record and establishes a new record of fifty-nine.

1923 Yankee Stadium opens. The stadium is called "The House That Ruth Built."

1926 Babe is the first person in World Series history to hit three home runs in one World Series game.

1927 The 1927 New York Yankees are remembered as "the greatest team in history." Babe Ruth and Lou Gehrig are in a home-run race. Babe sets a new record of sixty.

1929 Babe asks for a chance to manage the Yankees for the 1930 season. His request is denied.

Babe's first wife, Helen, dies. Babe marries Claire Merritt Hodgson.

1932 Babe "calls his shot" in a famous home-run hit at Wrigley Field in Chicago.

1935 Babe signs with the Boston Braves. In a game against the Pittsburgh Pirates, he hits his 714th, and last, home run. Soon after, Babe retires from baseball. His home-run record stands for thirty-nine years.

1947 April 27 is Babe Ruth Day at Yankee Stadium. Over sixty thousand people come to honor him.

1948 On June 13, Babe makes his last appearance in Yankee Stadium. On August 16, Babe Ruth dies.

For Further Study

More Books To Read

Babe Ruth. Rae Bains (Troll Associates)

Babe Ruth. Art Berke (Franklin Watts)

Babe Ruth. Norman L. Macht (Chelsea House)

Babe Ruth. William R. Sanford (Crestwood House)

Babe Ruth, Home Run Hero. Keith Brandt
(Troll Associates)

Baseball. Ray Broekel (Childrens Press)

Baseball Players Do Amazing Things. Mel Cebulash
(Random House)

The First Book of Baseball. Martin Appel (Crown)

*They Shaped the Game: Ty Cobb, Babe Ruth,
Jackie Robinson.* William Jay Jacobs
(Charles Scribner's Sons)

Video

Babe Ruth and Casey at the Bat.
(Children's Television International)

Babe Ruth: The Man, the Myth, the Legend.
(Fries Home Video)

Index

106